Endorsements

Kris S. Lee, MD takes you into the realm of Medicine through the eyes and ears of a resident physician. This book is a delightful read and exposes you to the idiosyncrasies used and practiced in a residency training environment that are not commonly exposed to the general public. It is an insightful script full of key information and unrestricted experiences for undergraduate and medical students interested in pursuing a field in primary care medicine.

Adolfo Aguilera, MD

Associate Program Director: Riverside University Health System (RUHS)/University of California Riverside (UCR) – Family Medicine Residency Program.

* * *

Engaging and entertaining vignettes take the reader into revealing moments in the life and times of physicians in training. Dr. Lee allows the reader to go into the trenches – to feel the emotions, taste the tension, inhale the challenges, see the joys, and smell the essence of what it means to be done with medical school and be called a doctor, but not yet ready to practice on your own. From hospital settings to outpatient clinics, this book will give you pearls of wisdom that anyone thinking about pursuing a career in medicine will treasure! Witty, informative, honest! Inside scoop to doctor talk! You'll want to finish the book in one sitting!

Sanjeev Nandakumaran, MD

Family Medicine Physician, Ambulatory/Urgent Care & Hospitalist, Southern California Permanente Medical Group.

Teaching Faculty at University of Southern California School of Medicine & Dentistry.

Champion for New Physician On-boarding & Clinical Patient Communication (Kaiser Baldwin Park Medical Center).

iNSiDELINGO MEDICINE

By Kris S. Lee, MD
Illustrations by Ju-Yeon Kim

www.InsideLingoBook.com

© May 2017, Kris S. Lee

All rights reserved. This book and all illustrations or parts thereof may not be reproduced in any form, stored in any retrieval system, or transmitted in any form by any means—electronic, mechanical, photocopy, recording, or otherwise—without prior written permission of the author, except as provided by United States of America copyright law. For permission requests, please contact the author at www.InsideLingoBook.com.

This is a work of fiction and any resemblance to actual persons, living or dead, or actual events is purely coincidental and not intended by the author.

The information in this book is in no way intended to substitute for the medical advice of your personal healthcare practitioner.

Illustrations by Ju-Yeon Kim.

Author photo by Helen Kim.

Cataloging information:

1. BUSINESS & ECONOMICS / Careers / General;

2. YOUNG ADULT FICTION / Comics & Graphic Novels / General;

3. MEDICAL / Education & Training.

ISBN 978-0-9990642-0-7

Printed in the U.S.A.

www.InsideLingoBook.com

Dedication

To my parents, Bob Lee and Kay Wu:

Thank you for loving me and nurturing me with everything you worked so hard for. Thank you for persevering through more than forty years of marriage. I love you so much.

To FS&HS:

I really get to do this??? Awesome!

Kris

Acknowledgments

Thank you to those who encouraged and supported me throughout this process.

Thanks to Dr. Adolfo Aguilera, MD; Dr. Megan Gaddis, MD; Curtis & Charlyn Hiebert; Belinda & Vassiea Hurt; Zoey Kim; Tawney Lee; Dr. Sanjeev Nandakumaran, MD; Nathan Shin; Dr. Shunling Tsang, MD and Tabitha Winesberry for reading the manuscripts and giving valuable feedback.

Special appreciation to Ju-Yeon Kim and her excellent artistic talent and unflagging professionalism in creating faces from my words.

Special appreciation to Helen Kim of www.TheThinkFarm.com for her photography skills.

Thanks to all my patients for letting me into your lives, and trusting me enough to let me "practice" on you.

To all my colleagues in the healthcare field, you are all amazing. Keep fighting the good fight.

And last, but not least, thanks to Adam Torres for inspiration and constant push. This book started because of you, "Dr. Torres"!

Table of Contents

Dedication v
Acknowledgments vi
Table of Contents vii
Introduction 1
Part 1: At a Teaching Hospital 3
    July 1st 5
    August 14th 19
    October 16th 23
    December 3rd 27
    January 9th 31
    March 27th 35
Part 2: A Morning at the Clinic 39
    May 22nd 41
Epilogue 53
Part 3: Appendix 55
A TO Z Glossary 57
The Road to Becoming a Doctor 75
Q&A about the book 79
Q&A about the author 83

INSIDELINGO
MEDICINE

Introduction

All industries have their own special language. To really understand what the insiders are talking about, you need to know their special code words: their InsideLingo.

In this book, I give you a glimpse into the training required to become a doctor (in Part 1: At a Training Hospital), and the daily pattern of work for a clinic doctor (in Part 2: A Day at the Clinic).

Throughout this book, you will see InsideLingo words marked with §. The definitions of the InsideLingo words will be in the 2nd half of the book. There is also an appendix with some more detailed information at the end of the book.

Enjoy your peek into their world: InsideLingo Medicine!

Mystery Alert!

There is a little mystery hidden in this book, related to the doctors' names. See if you can figure it out and let me know at www.InsideLingoBook.com.

Part 1: At a Teaching Hospital

Hospitals never sleep, and neither do the residents, students and nurses.

Follow the residents through a year at Springfield County General Hospital.

July 1st

7:22 AM. Springfield County General Hospital, 4 South.

Alex was in trouble.

It was 7:22 AM. He had two more patients to round § on, and he couldn't find the charts. Not that he necessarily needed the charts, because they had an electronic medical record § (See EHR/EMR). BUT STILL! There were only 8 minutes left until Dr. Williamson, the most feared attending § in Springfield County General, would walk through the badge-activated double doors. It was the 1st day! Everything had to be perfect!!

Bryan could see that he had to do something, and fast, but what? He and Alex were seniors § (See Resident) on the Family Medicine team § (See Appendix). And it was July: the worst time of the year. They were new, the interns were new, the students were new. Even the pharmacy and nursing students were new. There was mass confusion in the hospital. His regular morning duties of reviewing the blood tests and the results of studies done the previous day and visiting each patient had taken twice the time it should have normally taken. It was a wonder Bryan had finished seeing his patients. But he had gotten to the wards § more than two hours ago. And Alex, as always, had just barely squeaked in 25 minutes ago.

He was always saving Alex's hide. Alex was a good friend. He was fun to hang out with, always ready for a good time, and generous, almost to a fault. But he was hard to work with. Bryan put in his time, he kept his nose clean, he did everything right, and everyone could count on Bryan. When his teammates didn't or couldn't pull their own weight, Bryan was there to fix the mess before it got out of control. Alex seemed to never follow the rules. And he had gotten away with it until now. But now they were in charge. They were the seniors on the team. People's lives were at stake. Dr. Williamson was the attending! And it was the worst time of the year! And Alex still hadn't seen all the patients! Everything was starting off on the wrong foot!!

* * *

The energy of all the new faces on the wards was invigorating. Alex felt a little funny wearing a tie, but Bryan had convinced him it was important to show the students what their standards were. Bryan was definitely a spit-shined shoes and starch and iron everything kind of guy. Alex preferred to wear scrubs anytime he could get away with it; it was just like wearing pajamas at work.

Alex looked over at Bryan and gave him a thumbs-up and a huge smile, and motioned good breath in, bad breath out to remind him to breathe. Alex could tell Bryan was getting worked up. Bryan was such a rules and regulations guy for "a black kid from the hood". That's how Alex always teased Bryan. In reality, Bryan came from a well-to-do, multi-generational military family, and Bryan himself had served in the Army.

Poor Bryan, he still couldn't relax. It was their third and last year in residency (See Appendix). Top of the totem pole, some power, but really no true responsibility –

this was the year to really enjoy life. Bryan needed to learn to think out of the box, and be present in the moment.

Alex had been on the wards the night before – before the flurry of new student chaos landed in Springfield General. He had spoken with the nephrologist § (See Specialties) about Mr. Chang, and they had discussed the bioethics § of the organ donation system. Apparently in that part of the state, the decision about even doing HLA typing § was made at the university hospital by the transplant committee. He had reviewed Mrs. MacDonald's CT scans § with the general surgeon § (See Specialties). They had already spoken with her family; the family had decided against a biopsy § (See Treatments) since she was so old and her dementia was rapidly progressing. He had run the list § with the social worker § (See Specialties) and knew that Mr. Potts would likely need placement at a half-way house since his family would not accept him back at home, but that would have to be approved by his parole officer. He knew the charge nurse § and the pharmacists § (See Specialties) had the charts that Bryan was freaking out about, and those only had copies of previous ECG's § and generic hospital admission forms. Everything was under control.

* * *

Meanwhile in the security office.

In July, Doug Williamson liked to hang out in the security office in the morning, to watch the surveillance cameras. His 35+ years as a doctor had honed his skills in observing human behavior. These young kids: they never changed. A few were scared – easy to spot, they walked around in a 3-foot radius circle at the nursing station §, back and forth, like a little wind-up toy. Then there were the gunners § – yelling at the nurses, stealing charts from the pharmacists – no clue they were shooting themselves in the foot and making enemies of the best help they would have during their 2 years on the wards. The majority: eager, hard-working, traveling in packs of 3 to 5 – they wouldn't cause trouble, and wouldn't be memorable. Occasionally, you could see one or two: assertive, confident, watching, asking questions, listening and actually understanding – those were the interesting ones.

Then there were his residents. Ahh… his residents: Alex Zamora and Bryan Young. He had suggested they be the seniors of the medicine team in July. As third years, it was their last year under his wing. He wanted to make sure that they knew what they were doing. He needed them to have their game together for the rest of the year, and for the rest of their class. He had known at their interviews almost two-and-a-half years ago that they were natural leaders. They needed refining by fire to get them ready for the real world, and he, Doug Williamson, was the best attending for that job.

* * *

7:30 AM. 4 South.

Swoosh, clang! The automatic doors swung open, announcing Dr. Williamson like some sort of monarch. His substantial belly entered the ward first – even more noticeable since his hands were clasped behind his back. Nodding condescendingly at each nurse who would unwittingly half-curtsy as he walked past, he waddled a bit stiffly down the hall to the nursing station, where the 3rd and 4th year medical school students made a reverent semicircle around him.

Close, but not too close. You didn't want to be too easy a target, just in case the attending wanted to pimp § someone. To the students, he appeared as ancient history itself – like a hard-back book with yellowing pages you only find in the dungeon caverns of old libraries. A lanky frame covered with crepey, liver-spotted skin, xanthelasmas § that could have been in a medical textbook, and a belly that was the reward of too many hours working late, eating late, and not exercising. As he peered through his bushy eyebrows, he snorted hard to straighten out the hairs in his very expressive nostrils (he loved the effect that had, especially on the female students).

Doug had to postpone the morning pimping session for right now. They had a patient in a precarious situation waiting for them downstairs – the radiologist § (See Specialties) had paged him a heads-up. July was not the best time of year to be a patient in a teaching hospital §. It was like being in a hurricane that lasted for more than a month – they called it the July effect §. He would never forget the 3 weeks he spent as a patient at Springfield General after his heart attack and subsequent bypass. Even though it was in late July, it was still bad. He vividly recalled getting poked and turned and interrogated by every medical, nursing, and pharmacy student, intern, resident and junior attending in the whole hospital. Internal Medicine, Cardiology, Cardiothoracic Surgery, Nephrology, Infectious Disease… Dermatology § (See Specialties) for God's sake! Everything that could go wrong, did go wrong, but he walked out of Springfield General alive. OK, so his wife pushed his wheelchair – he didn't walk. But when he came back, he was walking. So he knew what it was like to be a patient. He knew what it was like to be a patient at his hospital.

Clearing his throat, he said, "Dr. Zamora…!"

"Yes, sir. Good morning," returned Alex affably.

Doug looked Alex over. No scrubs: unusual, but given the special occasion of the 1st day of July, Doug could understand it. But a tie? If he hadn't seen it himself, he wouldn't have believed it. Bryan's doing, Doug concluded. Alex is a good kid, always happy to oblige. It was certainly easier to hide a belly in scrubs. And wearing a red tie with a tight shirt was not a look that flattered Alex. The residents were forever teasing baby-faced Alex about his dad-bod, especially since he frequently reported his bench-press weight to anyone who would listen.

Alex felt suddenly self-conscious under Doug's gaze. Alex had wanted to accommodate Bryan, so he... dressed up. Alex looked down at his tie: red stripes, the one his mom had given him when he got into med school. He'd only worn it twice before: at the matriculation ceremony, and then at graduation. And today was the 3rd time.

He raked his fingers through his curly hair awkwardly as he looked back at Doug. He should send his mom a selfie; she'd really like that. The first thing his mom would say: Aww, baby, you're wearing the tie. The second thing: When did you last get a haircut?!?

Satisfied with his lightning fast assessment of Alex, Doug turned to Bryan.

"Good morning, Dr. Williamson, sir! It's a beautiful July morning! What a great day to be at the hospital!" Bryan spit out. Dr. Williamson always made Bryan a little nervous. Which meant he always said a little too much.

Bryan was impeccably dressed, as usual. Bryan stood taller than Alex, posture ram-rod straight, athletic and lean. Long arms, long fingers, long legs. Bryan's face was always serious, but today he looked like a scary drill sergeant. First day jitters, concluded Doug, always uptight. I've got to get him to relax. I'll encourage him.

"Dr. Young. I'm sure you've gotten everything in order…" So the old master pulled his entourage into gear. He slowly turned his body away from the nursing station, and as he did so, the gaggle of students followed in a wake around and behind him. He was the pilot of a small and fluid ship made of eager young minds and another two maybe not so eager, and a few years not so young. Doug was flanked by Alex and Bryan as they made their way to the ED §.

* * *

7:36 AM. Cafeteria.

Candice Xu was the night float §. Gosh, she hated being the night float! And it was July 1st! Technically she shouldn't be working, since she had officially graduated on June 30th, which was almost 8 hours ago. Her program wasn't malignant §, but they sure were ridiculous on some things. Why make her the last night float of the year? She was graduating! They could have made a 2nd year be night float the last 2 weeks in June…

At least the last 2 weeks had been pretty light. The hospital census was low because it was summer and everyone was on vacation. (People seemed to take vacation from being sick, too.) She had gotten to sleep several solid hours each night. Her intern § and students were all seasoned veterans by this point, so it had been a pretty breezy rotation § (See Medical school structure in the Appendix).

Her team was sitting around the table, chummy and chatty, finishing their breakfasts. Esther Verma was her intern. She had her hair pulled back in a messy bun and wore her thick, heavy glasses, with not even a smear of gloss on her lips. Jack and Linda were their students. Jack's face showed the imprint of the pillow case and his hair stuck up and out in the back. Linda's face was swollen and yesterday's mascara was flaking off her lashes. All were a bit disheveled and wearing scrubs, the typical post-call § (See Call system) look.

Candice sighed softly to herself. This was the last post-call breakfast she would have in this hospital cafeteria. This morning was the last time she would sleep in those call rooms § (See Call system). She was really going to miss everyone. She had gotten up a little earlier and changed into a business casual outfit, and had done her hair and makeup. She needed to say goodbye to everyone, and didn't want to look like she had just rolled out of bed.

She swept her straight black hair over her shoulders, and stood up to her full five feet, one and three-quarter inches' stature. She straightened her shirt, brushed off her skirt, grabbed her tray and said, "Let's go, kids." She gathered her intern (who was now a 2nd year) and students to head over to the ED. Dr. Williamson should be there in another 5 minutes or so. "Does your phone still have charge? Will you call the CT § (See CT scan) tech and see if Mr. Simons is done yet?"

* * *

7:43 AM. Emergency Department.

There were 12 people packed inside the curtains hanging around bed 9 in the ED.

"Mr. John Simons is a 73-year-old Caucasian male of Irish, Scottish, Polish, and French descent. He is a practicing Catholic. He has lived in Springfield county all his life. He is a widower for the past 4 years. He used to work in the manufacture of lawn care equipment, and has been retired for the last 8 years. He..."

"Jack, Jack," interrupted Candice. "Please skip to his current situation."

The newly minted 4th year student looked up from his papers. "Oh, OK, Dr. Xu. Uhh... Mr. Simons was 'B-I-B-A', § (See Acronyms) brought in by ambulance..."

Bryan coughed with impatience. Jack looked up, confused, then looked down again.

"Uh, he came by ambulance to the ER § because he started feeling weak suddenly in his legs and thought he might be having a stroke § (See Diseases).

"He has a past medical history of hypertension § (See Diseases) – which is well controlled, glaucoma § (See Diseases) – which is well controlled, diverticulosis § (See Diseases) – which is inactive, tinea pedis § (See Diseases) – which is very bothers..."

At this point, Bryan gave a very loud yawn. Jack looked up at Candice, who smiled and nodded for Jack to continue. Candice ribbed Bryan hard with her elbow.

Jack continued, "Which is very bothersome, but quote: 'not anything to write home about,' end quote. He has a remote history of tonsillectomy § (See Treatments) as a child and inguinal hernia repair § (See Treatments) at age 52. Upon arrival to the ER, Mr Simons's blood pressure was 142 over 84, heart rate was 78, respirations 14, temperature 98.2 degrees Fahrenheit, pain level 0. His weight is 192 pounds or 87 kilograms. His current medications are losartan § (See Treatments) 50 mg once daily, aspirin § (See Treatments) 81 mg once daily, 2 eye drops for glaucoma whose names he doesn't recall, and stool softeners and anti-fungal cream as needed. He has no allergies to food or medications that he knows of."

As Jack continued to read from his SOAP note §, Candice's phone rang, and she stepped away. "Hi, Dr. Quinn, yes, we're at Mr. Simons's bedside now..."

Alex was quickly skimming the chart on the computer, and trying to listen to Candice's half of the conversation.

Jack's voice continued. "...the CT brain was negative for an acute stroke or bleed..."

"Yes, yes. Yeah, that's what I thought. My intern was great on the exam. Mm hmm... they didn't tell you the MRI § machine was down early this morning? That's what they told me, that's why I ordered the CT..."

Doug cut in, "Great presentation, Jack. Thank you. You get to advance to 4th year." He smiled a beatific smile; the students didn't know if he were joking with them. "Dr. Verma, will you present your physical exam findings?" Doug called out the overnight intern.

As Esther detailed her exam, Alex knew Mr. Simons didn't have a stroke. He pulled out his phone. He thought Kyle was still on call... § (See Call system)

"Uh huh... uh huh... the MRI won't be up for at least another 3-4 hours?... Oh, Kyle's there with you! Thanks so much, Dr. Quinn. Tell Kyle I'll put in the formal consult § in a few minutes... Hmm... will you have Kyle call me? Yes, extension 7122..."

"Mr. Simons, I am Dr. Doug Williamson, I am the attending physician in charge of this team. Thank you for letting us barge in on you this morning. How are you feeling now?"

"I feel great. Other than feeling my legs numb, and my low back is starting to get a bit more numb. My hands are OK. Those two nurses," motioning to Candice and Esther with his left hand, "were really great. I had all sorts of people talking to me last night, but those two really spent their time."

"I'm glad to hear that, Mr. Simons," said Doug. "They're a very important part of my team. But they make me call them 'Doctor.' Dr. Xu, you spoke with the radiologist?"

"Yes, Dr. Williamson. Mr. Simons, do you remember earlier this morning, I told you that I needed to check your neck for a fracture? So we had you do the 2nd CT scan? It's showing that one of your neck bones is crushed. It's pushing on parts of your spinal cord. That's why your legs and back are feeling weak and numb. I'm going to have our neurosurgeon § (See Specialties), Dr. Kyle Park, or one of his colleagues, come by and talk with you. For right now, it's very important that you don't move your head or neck."

Candice continued to explain to Mr. Simons what would be happening in the next hour. Esther quietly got on a computer and started writing orders. §

Mystery alert!

Have you figured it out yet? Keep reading, and keep note of the doctors' names!

Tell your answer at www.InsideLingoBook.com.

August 14th

8:30 AM. Urgent care clinic.

Alex was in the urgent care §. Since it was still summer, it wasn't too busy, especially in the mornings. He looked at the schedule again; it was slowly starting to fill up as people checked in. It looked like there was a patient with a rash that was being vitaled § (See Vital sign). A second patient... asking for medication refill? This early in the morning? That was odd. They could go see their own doctor. Maybe they're traveling... The third patient... low back pain. OK. Just another day in the urgent care. The fourth patient... *Yersinia pestis*...??? § What? When did the Black Death arrive in Springfield county?

"Hey, Tom," called out Alex, as he walked to the receptionist desk. "What's with the 9:15 slot?"

"Oh, sorry, Dr. Zamora. I was trying to get the volunteer aide to help me, and something happened. I corrected it already."

* * *

9:13 AM

Alex knocked on the door and cracked it open. "Ms. Shelly Carmichael?"

"Mrs. And you can come in." Shelly smiled an anxious smile. She wore a very pink and very frilly baby doll top with matching ribbons in her hair. Her hands were resting on her lower abdomen. She looked like she just needed some fashion advice, not a doctor.

"Nice to meet you. I'm Dr. Zamora. What brings you to the urgent care this morning?" asked Alex, trying to keep a professional face.

Suddenly her face became ghostly white as she grabbed her abdomen tightly. "It just happened again! I don't know what's happening! I'm so scared!" Her eyes started to tear.

"Well, Mrs. Carmichael, why don't you try to explain to me what just happened?" soothed Alex.

* * *

9:27 AM

"Well, from everything I can check, it seems that your baby is doing fine. Since you recently passed your 1st trimester, you may just be feeling quickening § – when you first feel the baby move. I..."

"Do you think that's all it is? My baby is going to be all right??" Interrupted Shelly, as her eyes started to water again.

"I'm pretty sure baby is fine. What you're feeling could also be gas or indigestion. I see on the computer that you have your appointment with Dr. Nichols tomorrow at 2 PM for your regular well pregnancy appointment. I..."

"Yes, I do! I love Dr. Nichols! She is the best of the best! But I was just so worried! I thought my baby was going to die!" Now the spigots were fully open and she was bawling. "But you were wonderful! Dr. Nichols is wonderful! You..."

Alex handed her a tissue. "Mrs. Carmichael, you can always call the 24-hour advice nurse, they'll be able to answer your questions, so you don't have to worry all night. If you have cramping, bleeding, things like that, make sure you call right away. It's 24 hours."

"This is my first pregnancy, you know," she said, dabbing at her face. "My pregnancy has made me so emotional... I'm sorry to have put you through all this, Dr. Zamora." She was smiling again. "I'll make sure to see Dr. Nichols tomorrow."

October 16th

6:30 PM. Family Medicine department conference room.

Esther and Bryan are running the list.

"... Mr. Axelrod has been discharged, but his family hasn't picked him up yet. He said they'll probably come for him after 8. Hopefully the nurse won't call you for anything. So that's it for the patients. How's your night float been so far?"

"I think the students must be black clouds §. I've never had so many admissions before. At least Michael is a total gunner – he wants to do everything! I've been able to keep him busy. But tonight is his rest night!"

"Yeah, just look at our patient list! 20 patients! I feel bad for having to scut § (See Scut work) the students out all day long, but I just can't get everything done without them. The attending's even letting them skip lecture so they can help us."

"No new admissions tonight, OK, Bryan? Have a quiet night."

* * *

7:46 PM

"This is Family Medicine § (See Specialties), Dr. Young," Bryan was erasing that text from his pager.

"Hi, Dr. Young, this is Blessing, nurse on 5 North, I'm calling about Mr. Axelrod, in room 5521."

"Yes, is he still here? His family hasn't come yet?"

"The family is here now. But they say he has a rash. They want you to look at it before they take him home," explained Blessing. "It's on his back, on one side only. I think it could be shingles § (See Diseases). Can you come by?"

"I'll come see him," Bryan hung up the phone. "George, why don't you come with me, and Joe, you can stay with the intern and help him with the admission in the ER. We'll meet you there."

* * *

7:49 PM. 5 North.

"See, George, the rash is in the right T10 dermatome, § low back area and wraps around to the umbilicus §." The family was listening as intently as George was. "And the lesions § look like small blisters in clusters scattered all along that strip of skin. And it feels like what, Mr. Axelrod?" asked Bryan.

"It's burning, like someone is rubbing hot sauce on my stomach," the old man laughed at his own joke.

"OK, I'll give you a prescription for shingles, and Blessing will give you an informational pamphlet. When you see your doctor next week for your follow up, make sure you have him look at it again, to make sure it's healing well. By the way, have you had this lump for a while?" Bryan was grabbing a ping-pong ball sized lump on the left side of his belly.

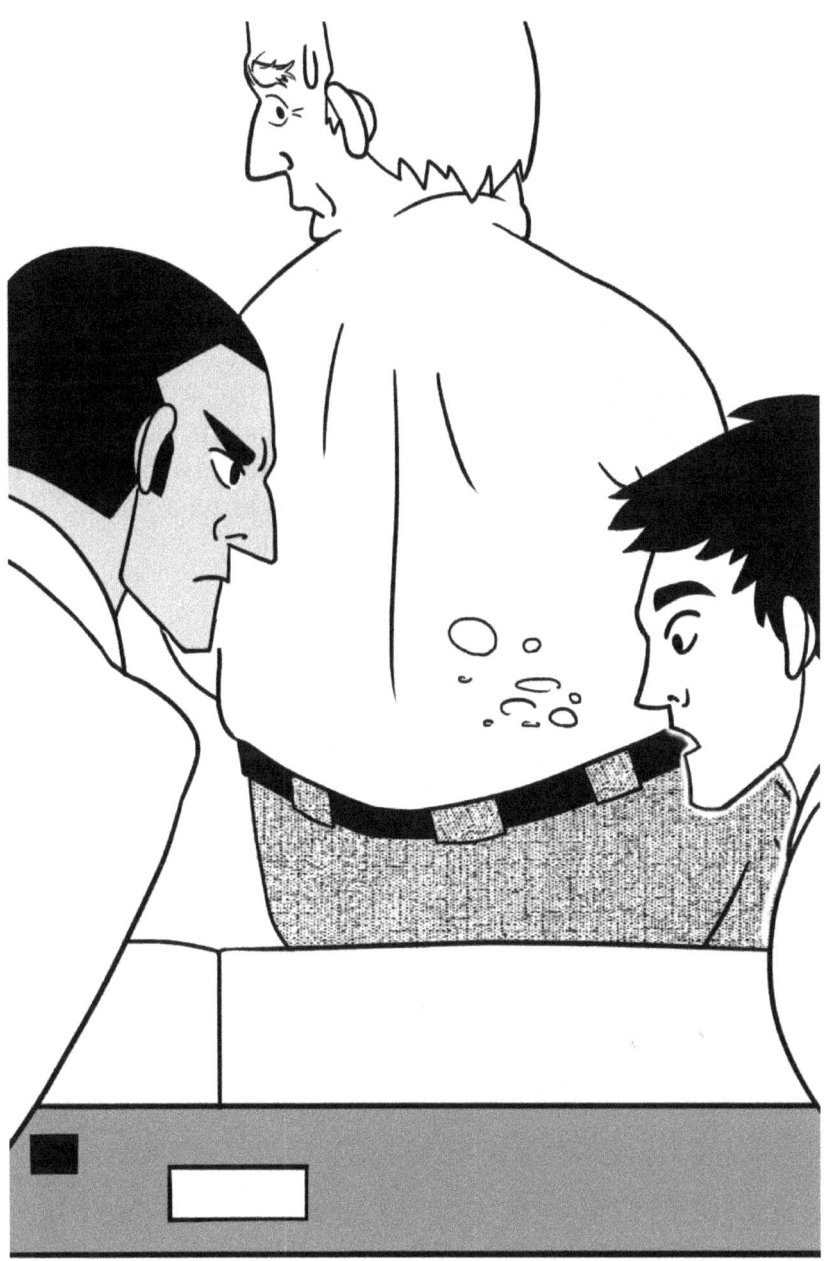

"Oh, yeah, my tumor! § I've had it for years, my grandson named it 'Bubba!' Ha ha ha!! Isn't he a hoot! When he was just a tiny tike! It doesn't bother me as long as I put my belt under it. It hasn't changed for, what? A decade?" he asked his family.

"Would you mind if my student felt that?" asked Bryan, then he motioned to George to feel the tumor. "See how soft and squishy it feels – like a lump of fat. And you can feel how it moves a little within the skin. It's a lipoma." And louder, for the patient and his family, "It's what's called a lipoma. It's a tumor of fat cells. It's not cancerous. But sometimes they can start to hurt, or grow quite large, especially if it gets irritated a lot. If it becomes bothersome, ask your doctor to refer you to the surgeon. They can remove it for you."

December 3rd

9:26 AM. Pediatrics clinic.

Dr. Hasina Sadiki is overseeing students in the Pediatrics § clinic.

"OK, Jack, I'm ready for you. What do you have?"

"OK, Dr. Sadiki, I have a 10-1/2-week old baby who is following up with his parents for the results of the karyotype § that Dr. Ulrich ordered 3 weeks ago. The results are normal," answered Jack.

"And why was the karyotype ordered?" inquired Hasina.

"Dr. Ulrich noted some issues at the 2 month well child checkup appointment." said Jack.

"Such as?" Hasina quickly countered.

"Uh... the mom said she didn't really know. Dr. Ulrich just ordered it," stammered Jack.

"Did you read Dr. Ulrich's last note? Did you examine the baby? Would you have ordered a karyotype?" grilled Hasina

"Uhh..." Jack had nothing to say. He thought this would be a quick in-and-out visit. He hadn't examined the baby. He just looked at the report that said it was a normal karyotype.

Hasina kept her sigh silent and stood up. "OK, Jack, Kelly, George. We will all go visit with this family. Monica," calling out to the secretary, "can you see if you can locate Dr. Ulrich? I think he is on Pediatrics inpatient § this month. Have him come down and wait for us; we should be out in about 20 minutes. Thank you!"

* * *

9:52 AM

Hasina and the students came out of the exam room. Frank Ulrich, intern, was waiting for them. She sat him and the 3 students down to review what had just happened.

"So, Jack – your takeaway today is...?" prompted Hasina.

"I need to examine every baby I get a chance to while I'm a student. The more practice I get, the better," said a chastened Jack.

"And Dr. Ulrich – your takeaway is...?"

"Have a really good reason for ordering a test, and understand the consequences of what it does to a family when I order something." Frank was crestfallen.

Hasina continued, "This is a very important lesson. Just because there is a test you can order, does NOT mean that you should order it. It does NOT mean it will give you the answer, or even AN answer. And when you do order something, make sure your patient understands why you are having them do the test. Think about what this family went through for 3 weeks – they thought something was wrong with their son! They thought it was their fault!

"That's why we have you think carefully about your Assessment and Plan § (See SOAP note). The question for this baby was, why is it not gaining weight very well? You jumped at a zebra § (See Zebra vs horse) diagnosis, Dr. Ulrich. You first looked for a chromosomal abnormality without having a VERY good reason. But you didn't look for the horses – poor feeding patterns, poor latching, diminished milk production: the common issues we see every day. Most of the time, you'll find your answers in your history taking."

January 9th

8:43 PM. Emergency Department

"Excuse me, are you Laura Kessler?" asked Esther.

"Yes," said the woman, through gritted teeth. "Who are you?" She seemed to be in a lot of pain.

"I'm Dr. Esther Verma, I'm with the Ob/Gyn § (See Specialties) department. And this is Kelly, our 4th year medical student. The ER doctor asked for a consult for possible admission. How are you doing?"

"I'm in pain! Can't you see that?" Laura snapped at Esther. "I can't believe I have to answer the same stupid questions 10 times to 5 different people..." she said to herself. "When are you people going to get me off this horrible gurney! I've been on this thing since 4 o'clock!"

Laura did look like she was in a lot of pain. Her hair was matted, her face was streaked with sweat, and her eyeliner was smeared and worn off. Esther tried to muster more compassion, but she was getting tired of being yelled at by patients and family members all day long.

In as professional a manner as she could manage, Esther said, "I'm sorry to hear that you've been here so long, Ms. Kessler. It is for your safety that we get as thorough a history as possible from you directly, and not hearsay from someone else. So, why don't you tell me what you've already told everyone else, and if I need more clarification, I'll ask a few questions." She mouthed over to Kelly that she would take the history from this patient.

* * *

9:04 PM

"OK, Ms. Kessler. We've gotten your history, I've examined you, my student has gotten the ultrasound report. We'll confer with Dr. Taylor and bring him down to see you as soon as he gets out of surgery."

Laura brightened up. "Did you say Dr. Taylor?"

"Yes," replied Esther. "He's our senior Ob/Gyn resident on duty tonight. He was in surgery when we came down. Once he's done, we'll present your case, and I think we should be able to return hopefully in half an hour."

"Take your time, take your time. No need to rush Dr. Taylor."

* * *

9:39 PM

"Ms. Kessler? It's Dr. Verma and Kelly. We have Dr. Taylor with us. May we come in?"

A sweet voice lilted out, "Yes, please. Please come in." Esther and Kelly shared puzzled glances. They opened the door.

Dr. Grant Taylor strode confidently across the room. He was built like a swimmer – broad-shouldered, trim-waisted – and sported a natural-looking tan even in the dead of winter. Everyone acknowledged that he was the most Adonis-like doctor in the whole hospital. The hospital administrators put him in the photos for all the

hospital's public events, and the local newspaper had featured him in their annual "Most Eligible Bachelor" article for the last 3 years, so his reputation had spread far beyond the walls of Springfield General.

His thick blond hair was attractively tousled, as he had taken off his surgical headgear a few minutes ago. Even in the harsh fluorescent light, his complexion glowed and those cheekbones were stunning to behold. His teeth flashed blinding white as he smiled. "Ms. Laura Kessler, good evening. It's a pleasure to meet you, only if it weren't under these circumstances... Have we met before? Have I taken care of you in clinic?" He held out his hand. Laura took it and giggled.

Laura had transformed herself in the half hour Esther and Kelly were away. Her hair was combed and gracefully laid across one shoulder. The greasy shine was banished from her complexion. Eyeliner, blush, and lipstick had been applied. She even looked like she had changed clothes, she looked so different. There was even the hint of a fresh floral scent in the room. Esther and Kelly looked at each other, mouths slightly agape. Wow, thought Esther as she pushed up her glasses, what a master, I should take notes...

March 27th

10:08 AM. Neonatal Intensive Care Unit (NICU).

"Dr. Zamora, did you make sure that the students have adequately sanitized their hands and stethoscopes?" Ian Ramsey, spoke slowly and methodically, as he glided his way between the rows of incubators.

"Yes, Dr. Ramsey. I made sure." Alex gave the students a mock threatening glare, then smiled.

Ian, the neonatalogist, § continued unnoticingly, "So, this patient is doing quite well." He proceeded to open up an incubator. "And I think she should be able to be discharged in the next few days." His soft, monotonous voice was harder to hear because he tended to speak into his chest. Alex motioned for the students to stand closer. "And I want the students to examine the patient," Ian began removing the baby's diaper. "I want to demonstrate the proper way..." he stopped short. "The child is defecating."

Upon hearing that, the nurse who was in the NICU quietly walked to the other side of the room.

"Dr. Zamora. If you would, please, fetch me a clean diaper." Ian seemed a bit flustered, but since he had been a neonatologist for well over 20 years, a diaper change was nothing new for him. Alex started to look under and around the incubator. The students started looking around, too.

The nurses had gathered together, just outside of hearing range, to watch. They whispered to each other, "How many doctors does it take to change a diaper?"

One answered, "Well, there's four here today, but none of them will get it right!"

Another giggled, "I bet you, it'll take them at least 15 minutes just to get that baby cleaned up!"

Part 2: A Morning at the Clinic

It is almost a year after Candice has graduated from residency, and she is working at a local clinic. Follow along with Candice as she goes through a typical morning's schedule of appointments. There's always something unexpected, and she's always running late.

May 22nd

```
Schedule for Dr. Xu, Candice
May 22

8:30 AM  Jones, Michael, 52, M. DIABETES FOLLOW UP.
8:50 AM  Cranston, Shirley, 68, F. PERSONAL ISSUE.
9:10 AM  Heder, Jeremy, 13, M. NEW PATIENT, POSSIBLE RASH.
9:10 AM  Carroll, Luisa, 81, F. MEDICATION PROBLEM.
9:30 AM  Brown, Carol, 43, F. SORE.
9:50 AM  O'Leary, David, 46, M. PER DR. XU.
10:10 AM Di Marco, Tony, 58, M. ONGOING COUGH.
10:30 AM Sanchez, Margaret, 39, F. 6 WEEK DIABETES FOLLOW UP.
10:50 AM Nguyen, Vu, 37, F. PERSONAL ISSUE.
11:10 AM Clark, Leslie, 28, F. RED EYE.
```

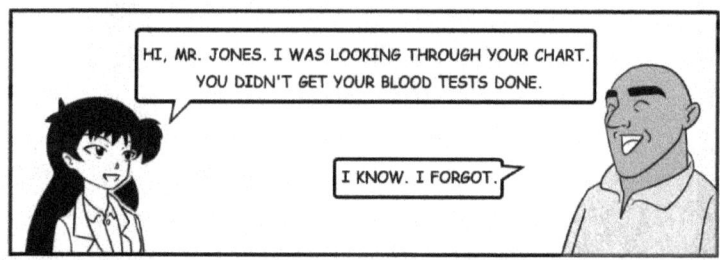

NOTE: A SUGAR READING OF 246 IS VERY HIGH. THAT MEANS MR. JONES'S DIABETES IS OUT OF CONTROL.

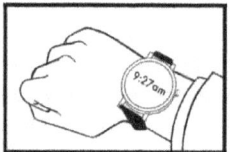

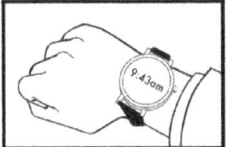

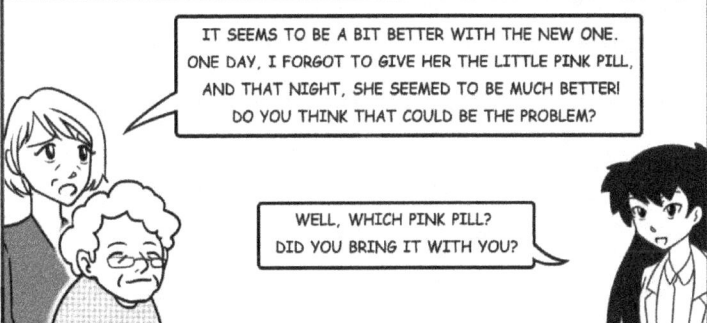

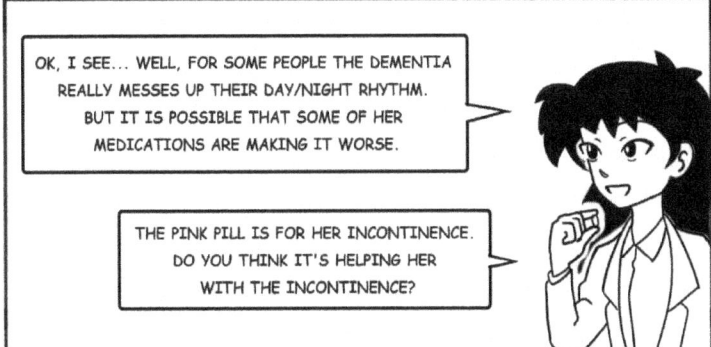

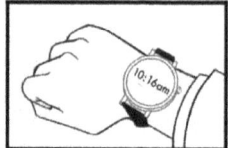

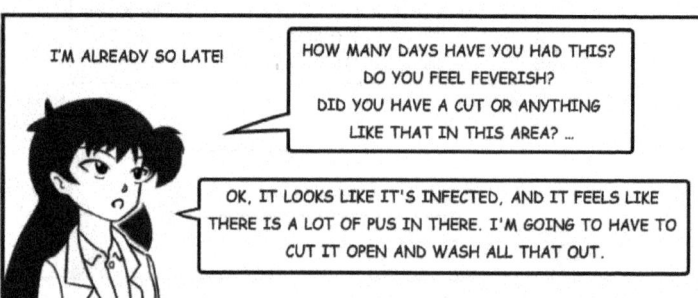

NOTE: SOMETIMES WHEN AN INFECTION HAS GOTTEN VERY BAD AND STARTED COLLECTING PUS, THE ONLY TREATMENT IS TO CUT IS OPEN AND WASH ALL THE PUS OUT. THIS PROCEDURE IS CALLED AN INCISION AND DRAINAGE.

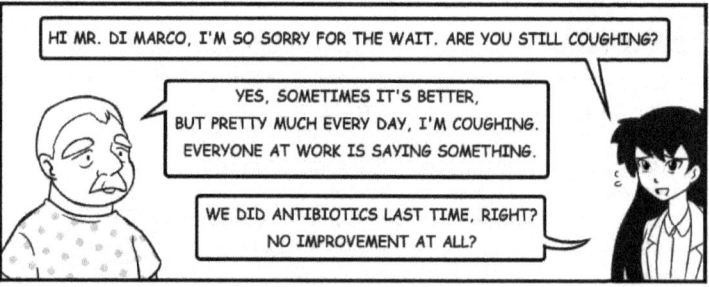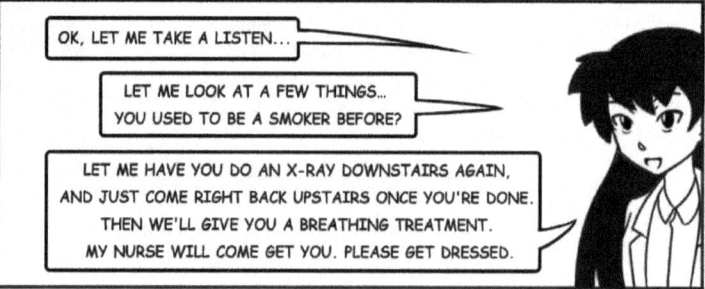

NOTE: A SUGAR READING OF 197 IS QUITE HIGH. THAT MEANS MRS. SANCHEZ'S DIABETES IS OUT OF CONTROL.

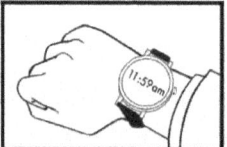

9TH PATIENT
10:50 AM APPOINTMENT.
NGUYEN, VU. 37, F.
PERSONAL ISSUE.

HI, MRS. NGUYEN, SORRY FOR THE WAIT. WHAT CAN I DO FOR YOU TODAY?

WELL, I WANTED TO TALK ABOUT GETTING INFERTILITY TREATMENT.

OK, LET ME START WITH SOME QUESTIONS. HOW LONG HAVE YOU GUYS BEEN TRYING TO GET PREGNANT NOW? HAVE YOU BEEN PREGNANT BEFORE?

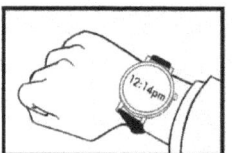

10TH PATIENT
11:10 AM APPOINTMENT.
CLARK, LESLIE. 28, F.
RED EYE.

HI, LESLIE. SO SORRY FOR THE WAIT.

IT'S OK, I EXPECTED IT, I'M YOUR LAST PATIENT FOR THE MORNING.

WHAT HAPPENED TO YOUR EYE?

WELL, I WOKE UP THIS MORNING AND IT'S SO RED, LIKE IT'S BLEEDING!

NOTE: IF YOU'VE NOTICED, CANDICE RUNS FURTHER AND FURTHER BEHIND AS THE MORNING GOES ON. THIS IS A GREAT SOURCE OF STRESS FOR BOTH THE DOCTOR AND THE PATIENTS. IF YOUR APPOINTMENT IS LATER IN THE MORNING OR THE AFTERNOON, EXPECT A WAIT.

Epilogue

The work never ends.

Candice will continue seeing patients into the afternoon, and maybe even into the night.

Alex and Bryan will graduate at the end of June and start work in other clinics or hospitals.

Doug will continue to train a new cadre of students and residents each year.

How about you? Would you like to be a medicine insider? Then continue to the Appendix and find out more about how to become a doctor.

Mystery Alert!

Did you figure out the mystery of the doctors' names? Do you still need a hint? Go back and check their initials. If you figured it out, let me know at www.InsideLingoBook.com.

Did you enjoy the book? I would love it if you left a positive review and shared it with your friends!

Part 3: Appendix

A TO Z Glossary

- A -

Acronyms

An acronym is the shortening of a phrase into the 1st letters of the words of the phrase, such as using "ER" rather than "emergency room". The use of acronyms is very common in medicine, since it is so much easier to write a few letters rather than write out the whole words. For example: **BIBA** = **B**rought **I**n **B**y **A**mbulance. **NCAT** = **N**ormo**C**ephalic, **AT**ramatic (means that the head is a normal shape and has no damage). **EOMI** = **E**xtra**O**cular **M**otion **I**ntact (means that the movements of the eyeball are normal).

Attending

In a training program, a title for the supervising, experienced physician who is ultimately in charge of the care of the patient.

In a non-training situation, the title is typically used in a hospital setting to refer to the doctor who is in charge of the care of one particular patient, the one who is "attending" to the care of the patient.

- B -

Bioethics

Discussing what is good or bad, moral or amoral, as it relates to medical procedures, treatments, etc. E.g. how to decide who will get the 1 donated kidney when there are 5 people who need the kidney.

Black cloud

This references the observation that certain people (residents, interns, students) always have a very bad call – lots of new patients, lots of very sick patients, lots of incidents and pages overnight. The person or team is the "black cloud" that brings bad luck.

(See Call system)

- C -

Call system, "on call"

Since it is impossible for someone to be constantly 24/7 awake and available to address issues arising for patient care, the call system assigns a doctor/resident to be "on call". This person is designated as the one to be called by nurses, paging services, etc., to handle questions that may arise overnight.

In a residency setting, this is typically the night float resident. Typically, the night float resident has a team of an intern and one or more students. For surgical services, the attending is frequently in the hospital as well, in case of an emergency surgery that might arise overnight.

There are sleeping rooms provided, called "call rooms". "Post-call" is the morning after an overnight duty, and residents are there to relay information to the day-time team that comes in to take over.

(See Attending, Night float)

Charge nurse

This is the nurse that acts as essentially the manager for the ward. Duties are more administrative (such as keeping track of what the other nurses are doing), rather than providing care directly to a patient.

Consult (short for consultation)

A patient typically has one doctor (or team) that is primarily in charge of his care. If the patient develops an issue that requires the input of a different kind of doctor, a consult request will be placed for a specialist to help take care of the patient along with the primary attending.

CT scan

Acronym for computed tomography. This is a way to image the inside of a body, by taking numerous x-rays which a computer reformats to show a cross-sectional image of the body.

- D -

Dermatome

This is a way of delineating the surface of the body according to the nerve that gives sensation to that portion. This becomes important when discussing diseases like shingles and disc herniations.

Diseases

Diverticulosis – a condition where the large intestine develops little pouches which can become infected

Glaucoma – a persistent elevation of the pressure inside the eyeball

Hypertension – a persistent elevation of blood pressure

Shingles – a rash from the virus that causes chicken pox

Stroke – where a portion of the brain is damaged by a lack of oxygen

Tinea pedis – fungal infection of the skin of the foot, commonly known as athlete's foot

---

- E -

ECG/EKG (used interchangeably)

Acronym for electrocardiogram. This shows the electrical activity of the muscle of the heart. The procedure involves placing several stickers on the chest, which are attached to wires. The ECG machine is then able to record the electric impulses.

ED/ER (used interchangeably)

Acronym for emergency department/emergency room. This is the most exciting place in the hospital. This is the place where you go when you think someone may actually die or suffer irreparable physical harm if he doesn't go to the hospital right away. If bad weather or a party will keep you from going, then you probably don't need to be in the ED. This is not where you go when someone has had a bad cold for a week. (Please just make a same day appointment with your doctor or go to an urgent care.)

EHR/EMR (used interchangeably)

Acronym for electronic health/medical record. This is all the data about a patient, in an electronic format, accessed by medical staff and caregivers. All this information used to be in a physical chart full of sheets of paper (often in a manila file folder). The transition from paper to electronic charts was a major shift in medical care.

- F -

Fire a doctor/ patient

If you don't like your doctor, depending on your insurance, you just change your doctor; that is how you "fire" your doctor.

The doctor, on the other hand, should go through a more formal process, where he tells you that he will not be providing your medical care anymore. As a matter of courtesy, the doctor will try to make sure that you have your required medications, etc., until you can find a new doctor. Frequently, there will be a formal letter sent to you.

- G -

Gunner

This is a (derogatory) name for students/residents who are always working very hard to be the top of the class. Most of the time, the gunner is just really motivated, or very smart. But sometimes, the gunner actually does malicious acts to make it harder for someone else.

(See Malignant)

- H -

HLA (human leukocyte antigen) Typing
This is the system whereby a transplant recipient and donor are matched. It involves checking the types of proteins a person's body makes – the more similarly the recipient and donor match, the more likely that the transplant will be successful.

- I -

Inpatient/outpatient
This describes the setting of the patient/provider interaction. Inpatient describes those who are admitted to the hospital. Outpatient describes those who are seeking care in a clinic setting.

Intern
The trainee who is in his 1st year after graduation from medical school (post graduate year or PGY) is called an intern, regardless of specialty. People who don't know refer to all doctors-in-training as residents, but technically, residents are only PGY-2 and beyond.

(See Resident, Post graduate training in Appendix)

- J -

July Effect
This is the purported rise of medical errors and deaths in hospitals/clinics during July due to the influx of new students. Previous studies have said this was a real

phenomenon, but more recent studies are saying it is difficult to prove if this is real or not.

- K -

Karyotype

This is the examination of the chromosomes (the structures that contain DNA within cells) to determine if there are any abnormalities that may explain a constellation of features/signs/symptoms noted in a patient. Typically this is done on children. An example of a chromosomal abnormality is Downs syndrome.

- L -

Lesion

This is a wonderfully useful word! A lesion is any ABNORMAL thing – a spot on an x-ray, a growth on the skin, a damaged area of the spinal cord. Calling something a lesion does not define it as a bad, but does identify it as something that is not the same as the surrounding area or not as it is expected to be. A lesion can be normal (e.g. a freckle) or can be dangerous (e.g. skin cancer).

- M -

Malignant

This word is typically used to describe a cancer that is spreading and growing. But it is also used to describe a residency program or attending that is especially harsh and demanding: "That Ob/Gyn program is so malignant. The residents hardly get to rest!"

MRI
Acronym for magnetic resonance imaging. A method to visualize the inside of the body which does not use radiation like x-rays. Typically used to image the brain and ligaments/tendons/cartilage.

- N -

Night float
This is the resident assigned to be in the hospital overnight to take care of patient needs during the night hours (~ 7 PM to 7 AM), and to handle the admission of new patients. It can also refer to the duty assignment (which can be a few days or 2 weeks or longer in duration).

Nursing station
This is the work area that is typically located at the entry to a patient ward, where you can find the nurses sitting, working, and chatting.

- O -

Opioid medication
Opioids are a class of medications that work to relieve pain. Unfortunately, they are frequently very addictive, and have other side effects such as constipation, cognitive impairment, and respiratory depression. The

increased prescribing of opioid medications has led to increased numbers of deaths from overdose, as well as manipulation and deception of medical personnel to obtain opioid medications to re-sell on the streets, the Internet, or elsewhere.

Orders

Orders are written by doctors, physician's assistants or nurse practitioners. Orders are carried out by nurses and ancillary care staff. Everything that happens to a patient in the hospital must be ordered by a clinician. Medications are obviously ordered by clinicians, but things like what patients get to eat, whether they are allowed to get out of the bed on their own, whether their bowel movements get recorded – these must all be ordered by clinicians to be able to be carried out by staff.

- P -

Pimp

The highly stressful and time-honored tradition in which more senior members of the medical team grill less senior members with unrelenting questions about medical trivia. It is stressful for the one being pimped, but apparently can be enjoyable for the pimper. The more malignant the program, the more frequent, unrelenting and trivial the questions. Pimping should be distinguished from the normal and useful question and answer didactic method.

(See Malignant)

Post graduate training/education (residency program)

This is hands-on, clinical training, that can range from 1 to 6 years (depending on the specialty), and starts after one graduates from medical school.

To obtain a medical license, all 50 states require at least 1 year of post graduate training (the majority require 2 years if you graduated from a medical school outside of the US). So, at the minimum, you are required to do your intern year in a residency program.

(See Intern, Resident)

www.fsmb.org/licensure/usmle-step-3/state_specific

- Q -

Quickening

This describes when a pregnant woman first notices the movements of her unborn child. She may describe it as feeling like fluttering or gas. This typically happens about 13 to 16 weeks into the pregnancy.

- R -

Resident

This describes doctors in the 2nd or higher year of post graduate training.

The senior is the highest-ranking resident on a team, and carries most authority and most responsibility.

(See Intern, Post graduate training in Appendix)

Round, rounding

Doctors who work in hospitals "round". They go around the hospital visiting each of their patients in their different rooms. Doctors who work in clinics don't "round", since the patients come to them.

Alternate usage: Table rounds

For the teams, sometimes it is more time-efficient to sit around a table, and discuss the issues each patient has, rather than walking all over the hospital to visit each patient. The same information is shared and discussed, but the benefit of actually seeing the patient and getting their and their families' input is lost.

Run the list

Reviewing the list of patients that a team is caring for.

(See Round, rounding)

- S -

Scut work

This term describes "menial" duties, passed down to the lowest person on the totem pole of a medical team. This may include transcribing prescriptions, delivering prescriptions to the patient wards or specimens to the laboratory, gathering supplies to do a dressing change, purchasing food or drinks for the team while "real" work gets done. Back in the day, it is rumored that residents would ask (order) students to do personal errands (like picking up the resident's dry-cleaning).

Usage: "Oh, the 3rd year students are always the scut monkeys." "My resident scutted me out so much yesterday, I didn't even get to participate in the surgery."

Specialties

There are general doctors – Family Medicine, Internal Medicine, Pediatrics and General Surgery. And there are doctors who work specifically on 1 organ system or field of study.

Cardiology – heart disease

Dermatology – skin disease

Family Medicine – general care for children, adults, pregnant women, elderly

Infectious Disease – diseases that are spread by viruses and bacteria

Internal Medicine – general care for adult population

Neonatology – care of newborn babies

Nephrology – kidney function disease

Pediatrics – general care for children

Tropical Medicine – infectious disease seen in tropical areas, frequently spread by mosquitoes

Cardiothoracic Surgery – surgery involving the heart and chest cavity

General Surgery – all general surgery

Neurosurgery – surgery involving the brain

Obstetrics/Gynecology (Ob/Gyn) – pregnancy and female organ issues and surgery

Orthopedic Surgery – surgery involving joints and bones

Social worker – help with social issues, financial problems, family dynamics, elder care, placement of patients, etc.

Pharmacist – management of medications

Note: There are many other specialties which have not been mentioned in this book. Social work and pharmacy are not medical specialties, per se, but are integral parts of the care team in any medical setting.

SOAP note

The typical format for relaying medical information in an organized fashion.

S – subjective: things the patient can tell you: age, ethnic background, medical history, what happened to bring them to the doctor, etc.

O – objective: what the clinician can observe and measure: vital signs, results of blood tests, radiological studies, etc.

A – assessment: what the clinician has decided are the problems to be addressed.

P – plan: the plan of action for the items identified in the assessment.

- T -

Teaching hospital

This is a hospital that sponsors and houses a residency program or allows any types of student training programs (nursing, pharmacy, etc.) to rotate through.

Team

There are multiple doctors and specialties that care for patients in the hospital. They typically do not share the care of one patient, unless a consultation has been requested. (See Consult) The team frequently is referred to by the specialty or the attending's name, or can be referred to by a color (Neurosurgery team, Dr. Carlisle's Orthopedics team, Purple Internal Medicine team). The team may be 1 doctor, a doctor and a nurse practitioner or physician's assistant, or a group of doctors/residents/students.

Treatments

Aspirin – a medicine to decrease the risk of heart attack or stroke

Losartan – a medicine to lower blood pressure

Steroids – used for many things, but in Mr. Di Marco's case, used to fight inflammation which can cause wheezing.

Of note, you should always name your medication with the dosage and how often you are supposed to take it

Biopsy – a procedure where a small piece of the organ is cut out, so we can look at the cells under a microscope to determine whether it is cancerous

Inguinal hernia repair – a surgery to close an abnormal opening of the layers under the skin in the groin area

Tonsillectomy – surgical removal of the tonsils (inside the throat)

Tumor

This refers to a lump on or in your body, typically caused by abnormal growth of the cells, but it could even be a collection of fluid. The tumor can be benign (not cancer), pre-cancerous (there are some changes that could become cancer later), or cancer.

- U -

Umbilicus

This is the technical term for belly button.

Urgent care clinic

This is available for people who are unable or unwilling to make an appointment to see their doctor in several days to several weeks. This is for urgent, but not emergent (i.e. life-threatening), medical needs. Typically there are no appointments, so you show up and wait your turn.

- V -

Vital sign

Traditionally, the vital signs consisted of pulse (how fast your heart beats), blood pressure, (a measure of how hard your heart is pumping), respiratory rate (how many times you breathe in one minute), and temperature. A fifth vital sign – pain intensity rating – was made popular in the late 1990's. Recently, use of the fifth vital sign has been blamed as one of the causes of the epidemic of opioid medication overuse and addiction.

Usage: "being vitaled" means that a patient is having their vital signs measured and recorded.

(See Opioid medication)

- W -

Wards

These are the patient-bed areas of the hospital, where medical, nursing, pharmacy students get practical, hands-on experience in caring for and dealing with patients.

Usage: "The new 3rd year medical students will be coming to the wards for the 1st time on July 1st."

- X -

Xanthelasma

These are yellowish deposits under the skin, seen around the eyelid area of certain people. These deposits are high in cholesterol and can be hereditary.

(Of note, the photos in medical textbooks are typically EXTREME cases of whatever is being demonstrated. Regular, run-of-the mill cases only slightly resemble what the textbooks show.)

- Y -

Yersinia pestis

This is the bacteria that is responsible for causing the Plague, or the Black Death. The bacteria are harbored by rodents and spreads to humans through flea bites. We now have antibiotics to treat this disease. According to the CDC, we still see a few cases of Yersinia pestis infection in the US every year (16 cases in 2015).

- Z -

Zebra vs. horse

A zebra is a colloquialism for a rare and exotic disease.

"If you hear hoof beats, think of horses, not zebras!" This maxim teaches students to think of common problems 1st. In the US, you are more likely to see a run-of-the-mill horse, rather than a rare and exotic zebra. So, if someone has a runny nose, slight fever, sore throat and cough for a few days, most likely it is a minor cold (a horse), and not lung cancer (a zebra).

The Road to Becoming a Doctor

(This applies to medical education in the USA.)

If you want to be a doctor, be ready to study a lot, and study very hard. Most people who even attempt to apply to medical school maintain a near 4.0 grade point average (GPA) throughout high school and college. In addition to maintaining that 4.0 GPA, future doctors are volunteering, doing multiple extracurricular activities, serving their communities in leadership roles, and making a name for themselves through doing and publishing research.

Preparatory education:

First, you finish primary and secondary grades and graduate from high school.

Then, you go to college, typically 4 years, could be more or less.

Then, you go to medical school, again, typically 4 years.

So, you are looking at 20 years of going to school (elementary school through college) before you start working at a residency program.

Medical school structure:

(This applies to allopathic schools only. There is another kind of medical school termed osteopathic, which teaches osteopathic manipulative technique as well as modern western medicine.)

Traditionally, medical schools begin with 2 years of classroom learning. How things work on a cellular level are studied in the 1st year - like histology, embryology, physiology, bacteriology. The 2nd year has more classes where human structures, disease manifestations and treatments are studied – gross anatomy, pathology, pharmacology, epidemiology, infectious disease, etc.

The next 2 years are the clinical years – the students spend their time in "rotations" - 4-12 week periods visiting and working in different clinical settings and specialties. They will mostly be in the hospital, but can be in small clinics outside of the confines of the university. All 3rd year students must rotate through a pre-set series of rotations: Family Medicine, General Surgery, Internal Medicine, Ob/Gyn, Pediatrics, Psychiatry, etc. So, during training, all doctors had to participate in surgeries, delivering babies, treating psychiatric patients, the whole gamut! During the 4th year, a student can select to rotate through specialties that interest them, in order to get more experience (like ER or Orthopedics or Dermatology), or just to do something a little exotic (like traveling away from their university to study something like Tropical Medicine). (See Specialties in Glossary.)

There are some medical school that mix things up, so this may not have been your own doctor's experience.

Residency:

Residency is what the training program is called. The doctors-in-training are called interns or residents. The hospital that sponsors and where most of the training happens is called a teaching hospital. Most of the actual work of patient care in teaching hospitals is performed by the residents. Residents are paid, but paid poorly.

Residency lengths vary with each specialty. For example, Family Medicine residencies last 3 years, whereas General Surgery residencies last 5 years. Some doctors choose to do further training called fellowships, which can be 1-3 years in length.

www.uwmedicine.org/education/Pages/specialties-subspecialties.aspx

(See Post graduate training/education [residency program] in Glossary)

Intern year structure:

The 1st year or PGY-1 (post-graduate year) can also be called the intern year. This is a year of learning the ropes at the hospital, the division of duties among different specialties and different ancillary staff, and being responsible for the care of the patient – but under strict supervision from senior residents and attendings.

PGY-2 and further structure:

From year 2 onwards, the resident has more responsibility and less supervision.

Q&A about the book

Why did you write this book?

In working with my patients and learning about what they did for a living, I realized that all forms of work are very meaningful. We spend so much time working. We derive our significance and value through the work that we do. Obviously, you make money with your work, but more importantly, you use your unique mix of talents and skills to create a product or service to give back to the world.

Your work can enliven or kill you, body and soul. It doesn't matter if you design aircraft, or make hand-beaded jewelry, or stock cans in a grocery store – it's important. Because it's so important, it's critical that you do something that you love, and that you're good at.

With the InsideLingo book series, I am celebrating the beauty and value of all kinds of work. I hope to educate young people about the fun and challenging aspects of the work they might want to do.

I think a book like this would have been very helpful to me. I am a pioneer in my family; no one else is a doctor. I had no understanding of what I was getting into when I started this career. That set me up for a lot of unrealistic expectations that hindered my growth and frankly, made me very unhappy. I had no idea what it was to actually work as a doctor: the day to day interactions, responsibilities and challenges of this field.

Tell us about your own path to becoming a doctor.

Notwithstanding my own appendix, many people's path to their destination is not a smooth, straight shot.

I started undergrad as a pre-med major, decided against it, left school early, worked in insurance and education and information technology, before deciding that I needed to pursue medicine again. I went to a foreign medical school called Ross University, where there were a lot of older students who were training for a 2nd career. I became a doctor relatively late in my life. If you really want something, don't let someone else stop you. The detours make your journey uniquely your own, and can make you all the better for them.

Your characters are very culturally diverse – do you want to comment on that?

I only reflected what has been my personal experience. My context was a non-traditional medical school and working in Southern California; my colleagues and patients were of all ethnicities and cultural backgrounds. As I started writing, I only had a message in mind. But as I continued writing and really fleshing out the characters, I decided that I wanted to reflect the diversity in my own experience by making the characters of many different backgrounds. I believe that this is the reality in the medical field now.

What is the worst part about being a doctor?

Being a doctor is high stress, demanding work. The reality is, almost no one comes to see the doctor because they want to. They come because something bad happened, like an accident, or something in their body is changing or causing pain and it's scaring them, or I made them do tests and now they have to face the music and see how they did on the test. People are nervous and afraid, and often act angry and uncooperative. They come with a list of what they want, and I want to deliver good customer service, but I must also do my duty as the doctor and do what is needed. I have to order expensive tests and painful procedures. I frequently have to deliver bad news. I get 15-20 minutes to do all this. And depending on the day, I get to do this 20-40 times.

What is the best part about being a doctor?

It's humbling to think about how much trust I automatically received because of my title as a doctor. Having met me for the first time, a patient would allow me access to his body and tell me things he didn't share with most people, just because I was the doctor.

Q&A about the author

What do you like to read?

I have always loved to read: The story is told that I would sit on the floor with a bunch of manga, and pore over them, laughing away. That was at 5-6 years old. Whether I was actually reading or just enjoying the pictures, my mom and I both don't know. But I did memorize all the words in a picture book I had. When someone would ask me what a word was, I would start at the beginning of the book, recite everything until I got to the word, then I would tell them what the word was! (And no, I don't remember the words anymore...)

I prefer to read fiction for children. I love coming of age stories like Anne of Green Gables and A Wrinkle in Time. I read all the Black Stallion books I could find when I was in elementary school. I tend to wander into the children's section in libraries and bookstores to look at the children's books with the beautiful illustrations. I like to read non-scary mysteries, as well as adult educational material: financial, career development, personal growth and spiritual.

Tell us about your background.

My family immigrated from South Korea to Southern California when I was 6. I had all my schooling in the US except for a few months of kindergarten in Korea before we immigrated. Since then, I have lived in Southern California except for the 4 years of medical school when I studied in the Caribbean and in several states on the East Coast.

I got an F in English in the 1st grade, but I went on to graduate among the top of my class in high school, college and med school. And now I've written a book! One failure (or even several) doesn't automatically disqualify you from a goal.

So why do you like construction cranes?

I remember in elementary school, watching the Flintstones cartoon, wanting to be like Fred Flintstone when I grew up, and operate heavy machinery!

Some people like licorice (I don't like licorice). I happen to like construction cranes. Something about how they stand high above everything appeals to me. I think the outline of the metal rods against the sky is quite striking and beautiful.

Closing

Thank you for reading my book. I hope you enjoyed it and learned something useful. If there is an industry you'd like to learn more about, let me know at www.InsideLingoBook.com.

Sign up for email updates to find out about the next book in the InsideLingo book series!

www.ingramcontent.com/pod-product-compliance
Lightning Source LLC
Chambersburg PA
CBHW071309040426
42444CB00009B/1936